W9-BAM-547

Welcome to Mexico

By Mary Berendes

Welcome to the WORLD

Published by The Child's World®
1980 Lookout Drive
Mankato, MN 56003-1705
800-599-READ
www.childsworld.com

Content Adviser: Professor Gichana C. Manyara, Department of Geography, Radford University, Radford, VA
Design and Production: The Creative Spark, San Juan Capistrano, CA
Editorial: Emily J. Dolbear, Brookline, MA
Photo Research: Deborah Goodsite, Califon, NJ

Cover and title page photo: Steve Vidler/SuperStock
Interior photos: Alamy: 6 (Kim Karpeles), 14, 30 (Robert Fried), 20 (Russell Gordon/Danita Delimont), 22 (Hemis); Animals Animals: 7 (Manfred Gottschalk/Earth Scenes); AP Photo: 25 (Guillermo Arias); Corbis: 13 (Buddy Mays), 3, 17 (Guido Cozzi/ Atlantide Phototravel), 26 (Lindsay Hebberd); Getty Images: 12 (Susana Gonzalez/AFP), 18 (Wesley Bocxe/Newsmakers); iStockphoto.com: 24 (Charles Taylor), 27 (Chris Ronneseth), 28 (Ufuk Zivana), 29 (Andres Balcazar), 31 (Ian Johnson); Landov: 3, 19 (Tomas Bravo/Reuters), 21 (Luis Reyes/Reuters); Minden Pictures: 9 (Konrad Wothe); Mira.com: 10 (Cosmo Condina), 15 (David Sanger); NASA Earth Observatory: 4 (Reto Stockli); Oxford Scientific: 3, 8 (Robin Bush), 16 (Charles Bowman), 23 (Kathy Tarantola/ Index Stock Imagery).
Map: XNR Productions: 5

Library of Congress Cataloging-in-Publication Data
Berendes, Mary.
   Welcome to Mexico / by Mary Berendes.
      p. cm. — (Welcome to the world)
   Includes index.
   ISBN-13: 978-1-59296-920-3 (library bound : alk. paper)
   ISBN-10: 1-59296-920-8 (library bound : alk. paper)
   1. Mexico—Juvenile literature. I. Title.
F1208.5.B38 2007
972—dc22
                                               2007005560

Contents

Where Is Mexico?

Imagine that you could fly high above Earth. What do you think you would see? If you looked down, you would see some huge land areas surrounded by water. These land areas are called continents. Some continents are made up of many different countries. Mexico is a country on the continent of North America.

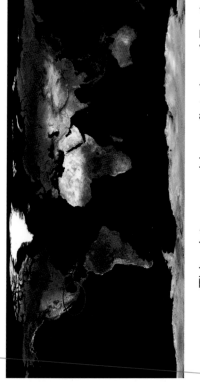

This picture provides a flat view of Earth. Mexico is inside the red circle.

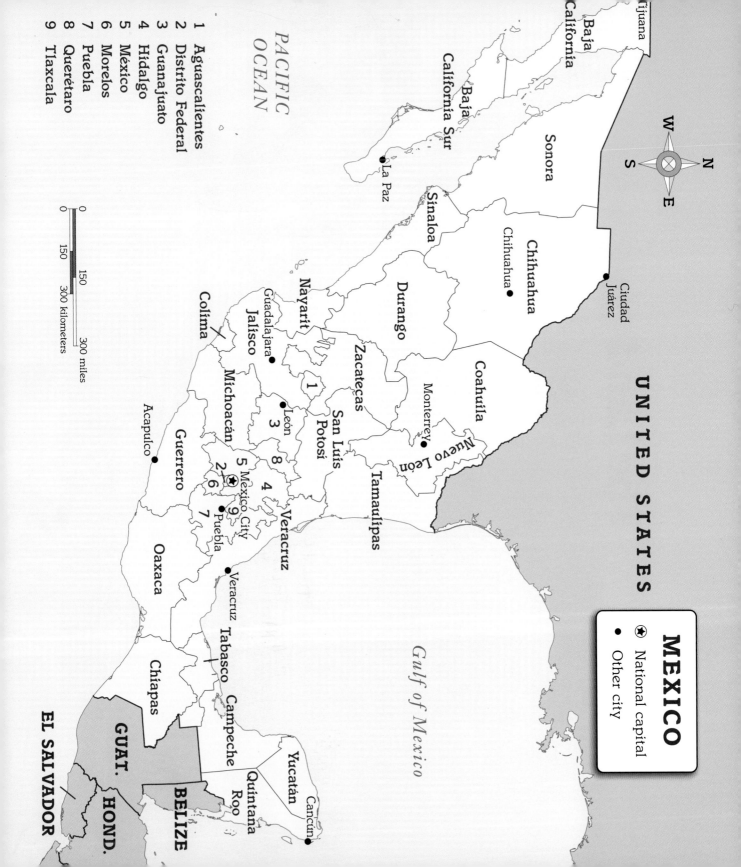

MEXICO

⊛ National capital
● Other city

1 Aguascalientes
2 Distrito Federal
3 Guanajuato
4 Hidalgo
5 México
6 Morelos
7 Puebla
8 Querétaro
9 Tlaxcala

PACIFIC OCEAN

UNITED STATES

Gulf of Mexico

Baja California

Baja California

Baja California Sur

Tijuana

Sonora

Chihuahua

Chihuahua ●

Ciudad Juárez ●

Coahuila

Monterrey ●

Nuevo León

Tamaulipas

Sinaloa

Durango

Zacatecas

San Luis Potosí

La Paz ●

Nayarit

Colima

Jalisco

Guadalajara ●

1

León ●

Michoacán

3

8

5

2

6

9

4

Mexico City ⊛

Puebla ●

7

Veracruz

Guerrero

Acapulco ●

Oaxaca

Veracruz ●

Tabasco

Campeche

Chiapas

Yucatán

Cancún ●

Quintana Roo

BELIZE

GUAT.

HOND.

EL SALVADOR

0   150   300 miles
0   150   300 kilometers

N
W   E
S

The Land

There are many different kinds of land in Mexico. There are mountains and jungles. There are plains and deserts. There are even beaches.

Much of Mexico is a huge, flat area called a **plateau**. A plateau is an area of land that is higher than the areas of land around it.

A man walks along a beach in Cabo San Lucas.

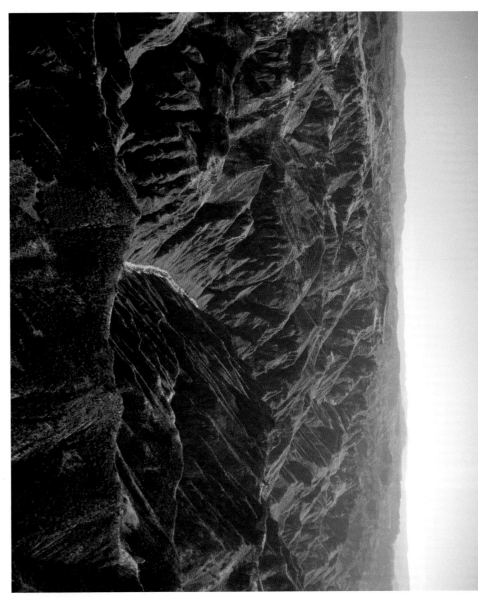

Sierra Madre means "mother range" in Spanish.

Mexico's plateau is bordered by two chains of mountains. One chain is in the west and the other one is in the east. They are called the Sierra Madre.

Plants and Animals

Many types of plants live in Mexico. Cactus and mesquite plants grow in the dry north. Thick jungles cover the land in other areas of Mexico. Oak and pine trees grow high in the mountains.

Just like the plants, the animals that live in Mexico are different in each part of the country. Wolves and coyotes are found in the north. Jaguars, bears, and pumas roam in the mountain forests. Colorful birds, snakes, monkeys, and lizards live in Mexico's jungles. Many types of insects and fish can be found in Mexico, too.

A keel-billed toucan in central Mexico

The giant cardon cactus grows in the deserts of Baja California.

Chichén Itzá is an ancient Mayan city in the Yucatán state.

Long Ago

Ancient Indian groups came to Mexico thousands of years ago. They included the Olmec, the Toltecs, the Maya, and the Aztecs. These groups built huge cities out of stone. They built **pyramids** and palaces and temples. They were so good at building, some of the things they built are still standing today!

In the 1500s, explorers from other countries began arriving in Mexico. They were looking for riches and for new places to live. Some explorers from Spain told their king about the beautiful land. He wanted Mexico to be a part of his kingdom. The country of Spain took away the land from the Indian groups.

Spain ruled Mexico for 300 years. The Mexicans fought back in 1810. Spain recognized their independence in 1821.

11

Mexico Today

Today, Mexicans have their own government. They have a president instead of a king. The president and the government make laws that keep Mexico safe. But only one group ruled in Mexico for many years. Finally in 2000, Mexicans voted for a member of a different group to lead them. It was an important day for Mexican freedom.

A political gathering in Mexico City in 2006

The Mexican people try to get along with one another. But not all people are treated fairly. Many Indians are forced to live in poor areas where they cannot get good jobs. To help, the government has given Indians some of the land their relatives once owned. But these areas are still very poor. Many people who live there work in coffee or vegetable fields to make enough money to live.

An Indian girl walks barefoot near her village in Chihuahua.

Mexican girls take part in a festival in Oaxaca.

The People

The Mexican population is made up of three groups. The Spanish people are relatives of the first Spanish settlers. The Indians are another group. The people in Mexico who have both Indian and Spanish relatives are called **mestizos.** Most Mexicans are mestizos.

Most people in Mexico live on the plateau or in the mountains. Areas that are close to the United States or along beaches are growing. In these areas, Mexicans can find lots of jobs to do. They can also find places to build new homes.

A mestizo at his shop in San José del Cabo

15

City Life and Country Life

Most Mexicans live in the city. In the city, people can find jobs to do and places to buy things. Hundreds of people move into Mexico's cities every day. Sometimes, Mexico's cities are so crowded, there are not enough places for the newcomers to live.

Many country people live in villages. They build houses with sticks and mud. Some people make their houses out of **adobe.** Adobe is a type of brick that is made from mixing straw with mud. Many country people work on farms. Others travel to the cities to work.

Mexico City is one of the world's largest cities.

Adobe buildings in an old mining town called Real de Catorce

Schools and Language

Mexican children begin school at the age of four. They attend two years of preschool and kindergarten. When children turn six years old, they begin elementary school. They learn math, science, and social studies just as you do. Most students in Mexico go to school until they are 15 years old. Mexico also has hundreds of colleges and universities.

Mexico's official language is Spanish. It was brought over by the Spanish explorers. Many Mexicans speak Indian languages in their villages. The languages of Mexico are very old and very beautiful.

Schoolchildren in Mexico work on computers.

Did you know?

Mexico is the largest Spanish-speaking country in the world.

Young Mexicans have fun together.

A worker finishes putting together an automobile in Hermosillo.

Work

In Mexico, there are many jobs to do. Some people work on farms that produce coffee, corn, beans, or fruit. Some people work in shops, hotels, and restaurants. Others make blankets and pottery to sell to Mexico's many visitors.

Mexico sells gas and oil to other countries. It is also a leading seller of silver in the world. And Mexico's cities have factories that make everything from cars to clothes. Mexico is a busy place!

A Mexican artist finishes a piece of pottery.

Food

Many dishes in Mexico are made with **tortillas.** Tortillas are thin, round breads made of cornmeal or wheat flour. They are used in dishes such as tacos and enchiladas. Many Mexican dishes are made with beans, corn, tomatoes, and peppers.

In Mexico, eating slowly and enjoying your food is very important. Meals are a time to relax and talk with friends and family. The biggest meal of the day is lunch. It is eaten around two o'clock in the afternoon. A light supper is served just before bedtime.

Did you know?

Mexico's Aztecs introduced chocolate to the rest of the world. In 1519, they served Spanish explorers a drink made from cacao beans (left). Then the Spanish shipped these beans back to Europe.

Mexican women make tortillas in a restaurant kitchen.

Pastimes

Mexicans love sports, especially soccer. They also like to watch baseball, boxing, and a fast game similar to racquetball called jai alai (HIGH LIE).

One of the oldest sports in Mexico is bullfighting. In this pastime, a man—or sometimes a woman—called a *matador* stands in a ring with a bull. The matador waves a bright cape at the bull, hoping the bull will charge. When it does, the matador quickly moves out of the way.

Did you **know?**

Mexicans hang **piñatas** (peen-YAH-tuhs) from long strings for special days. A piñata (right) is a brightly colored container filled with toys and candy. Blindfolded children try to hit the piñata with a stick. When the piñata breaks, toys and candy spill out for everyone to enjoy!

24

A matador performs during a bullfight in Guadalajara.

Bullfighting takes bravery and skill. If the matador moves the wrong way, the bull can hurt him. Some people think bullfighting is cruel because the bull usually dies at the end of a fight. These days, bullfighting is more of a show than a sport.

25

Holidays

Mexicans celebrate many of the same holidays as we do. One special holiday is the Day of the Dead. It is celebrated from October 31 to November 2. During this time, people remember loved ones who have died. They bake special bread, eat candy skeletons, and have picnics in cemeteries. In Mexico, the Day of the Dead is a time to remember the dead with joy instead of sadness.

Mexico is a beautiful country filled with bright colors and friendly people. Perhaps one day you will climb to the top of an ancient pyramid built by Indians. Or maybe you will want to visit one of Mexico's sunny beaches. Wherever you go, and whatever you do, Mexico is sure to make you smile.

A girl carries a basket of flowers in a Day of the Dead celebration.

26

Mexico City is home to the largest church in Latin America—the famous Metropolitan Cathedral, or *Catedral Metropolitana.*

Fast Facts About Mexico

Area: 761,600 square miles (1,972,550 square kilometers)—a little less than three times the size of Texas

Population: About 107 million people

Capital City: Mexico City

Other Important Cities: Guadalajara, Monterrey, Puebla, León, Ciudad Juárez, Tijuana, and Acapulco

Money: The Mexican peso

National Language: Spanish. There are also many Indian languages, including Mayan, Nahuatl, and other native local languages.

National Holiday: Independence Day on September 16 (1810)

National Flag: Three equal stripes of red, white, and green. The white stripe has the national coat of arms in the middle.

Head of Government: The president of Mexico

Head of State: The president of Mexico

Famous People:

Luis Barragán: architect

Carlos Chávez: composer and conductor

Benito Juárez: president of Mexico from 1861 to 1865 and 1867 to 1872

Frida Kahlo: painter

Montezuma II: last Aztec emperor of Mexico

Octavio Paz: winner of the Nobel Prize for Literature in 1990

Diego Rivera: muralist

Carlos Santana: rock musician

Fernando Valenzuela: baseball player

Pancho Villa: bandit and general

Emiliano Zapata: revolutionary and champion of the rural poor

National Song: "National Anthem of Mexico" (or "*Himno Nacional de Mexico*"). Poet Francisco González Bocanegra wrote the words to this song, which officially became the national song in 1943.

CHORUS
Mexicans, when the war cry is heard
Have sword and bridle ready.
Let the earth's foundations tremble
At the loud cannon's roar.

May the divine archangel crown your brow,
Oh fatherland, with an olive branch of
    peace
For your eternal destiny has been written
In heaven by the finger of God.
But should a foreign enemy
Dare to profane your soil with his tread,
Know, beloved fatherland, that heaven
    gave you
A soldier in each of your sons.

CHORUS

Fatherland, oh fatherland, your sons vow
To give their last breath on your altars,
If the trumpet with its warlike sound
Calls them to valiant battle.
For you, the garlands of olive,
For them, a glorious memory.
For you, the victory laurels,
For them, an honored tomb.

CHORUS

Mexican Folklore:

The Founding of Mexico City

Spaniards founded Mexico City in 1521. They built where the former Aztec capital city, Tenochtitlán (ten-osh-teet-LAHN), had been. Legend says the Aztecs chose the spot after an eagle landed on a cactus on an island in Lake Texcoco. The eagle carried a snake in its beak. The story fulfilled an Aztec prediction of the future, and marked the site for their new city.

How Do You Say...

ENGLISH	SPANISH	HOW TO SAY IT
hello	hola	OH-lah
good-bye	adios	ah-dee-OHSS
please	por favor	POR fah-VOR
thank you	gracias	GRAH-see-uhs
one	uno	OO-no
two	dos	DOHS
three	tres	TRACE
Mexico	México	MEH-hee-koh

Glossary

adobe (uh-DOH-bee) Adobe is a brick that is made from mud and straw. In Mexico, some people build houses out of adobe.

mestizos (meh-STEE-zohs) Mestizos are Mexicans who have both Indian and Spanish relatives. Most Mexicans are mestizos.

piñatas (peen-YAH-tuhz) Piñatas are decorated containers filled with toys and candy that blindfolded children try to break open with a stick. Mexicans hang piñatas for special days.

plateau (pla-TOH) A plateau is a huge, flat area that is higher than the land around it. Mexico's plateau is bordered by the Sierra Madre.

pyramids (PEER-uh-midz) Pyramids are ancient stone structures usually with a square base and four triangles that meet in a point at the top. Indians built pyramids in Mexico.

tortillas (tor-TEE-yahz) Tortillas are thin, round breads made of cornmeal or wheat flour. Tortillas are part of many Mexican dishes.

Index

Further Information

Read It

Gruber, Beth. *National Geographic Countries of the World: Mexico.* New York: National Geographic Children's Books, 2006.

Lourie, Peter. *Hidden World of the Aztec.* Honesdale, PA: Boyds Mills Press, 2006.

Sheen, Barbara. *Foods of Mexico.* Detroit, MI: KidHaven Press, 2006.

Stein, R. Conrad. *Mexico.* New York: Children's Press, 2007.

Look It Up

Visit our Web page for lots of links about Mexico:
http://www.childsworld.com/links

Note to Parents, Teachers, and Librarians: We routinely verify our Web links to make sure they are safe, active sites—so encourage your readers to check them out!